MAMMA MIA! ™

THE MOVIE SOUNDTRACK FEATURING THE SONGS OF ABBA®

ISBN 978-1-4234-6133-3

HAL•LEONARD®
CORPORATION

7777 W. BLUEMOUND RD. P.O. BOX 13819 MILWAUKEE, WI 53213

Visit Hal Leonard Online at
www.halleonard.com

HONEY, HONEY

Words and Music by BENNY ANDERSSON,
BJÖRN ULVAEUS and STIG ANDERSON

Hon - ey, hon - ey, how ___ you thrill ___ me, a - ha, hon - ey, hon - ey.
Hon - ey, hon - ey, let ___ me feel ___ it, a - ha, hon - ey, hon - ey.
Hon - ey, hon - ey, touch ___ me, ba - by, a - ha, hon - ey, hon - ey.

Hon - ey, hon - ey, near - ly kill ___ me, a -
Hon - ey, hon - ey, don't ___ con - ceal ___ it, a -
Hon - ey, hon - ey, hold ___ me, ba - by, a -

ha, hon - ey, hon - ey.   I'd heard a - bout you ___ be - fore,
ha, hon - ey, hon - ey.   The way that you kiss ___ good - night,
ha, hon - ey, hon - ey.   You look like a mov - ie star,

MONEY, MONEY, MONEY

Words and Music by BENNY ANDERSSON
and BJÖRN ULVAEUS

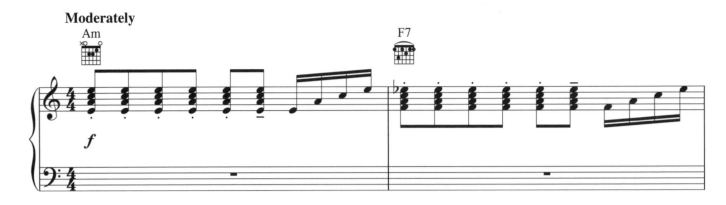

I work all night, I work all day to pay the bills I have to pay.

Mon - ey, mon - ey, mon - ey   must be fun - ny   in a rich man's world. _

_   Mon - ey, mon - ey, mon - ey   al - ways sun - ny

in a rich man's world. ___   A - ha ____

MAMMA MIA

Words and Music by BENNY ANDERSON,
BJÖRN ULVAEUS and STIG ANDERSON

DANCING QUEEN

Words and Music by BENNY ANDERSSON,
BJÖRN ULVAEUS and STIG ANDERSON

LAY ALL YOUR LOVE ON ME

Words and Music by BENNY ANDERSSON
and BJÖRN ULVAEUS

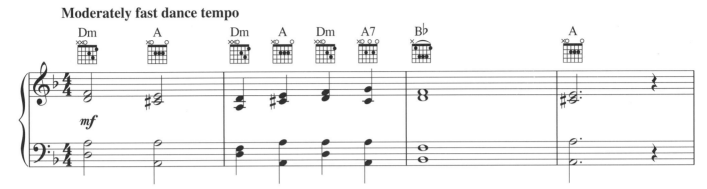

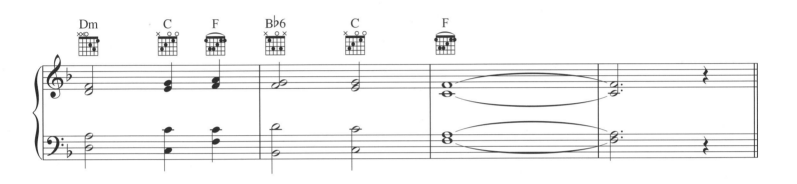

I was-n't jeal-ous be-fore we met,
It was like shoot-ing a sit-ting duck,
I've had a few lit-tle love af-fairs,

To Coda

D.S. al Coda

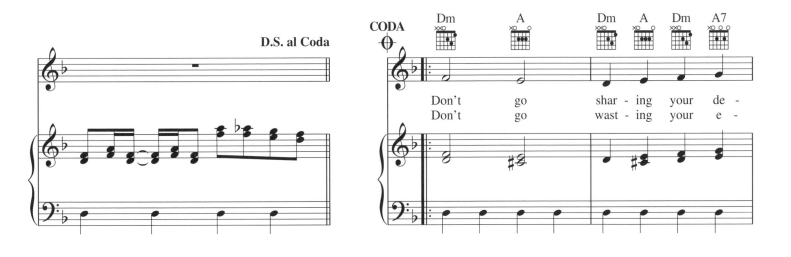

CODA

Don't   go   shar - ing   your   de -
Don't   go   wast - ing   your   e -

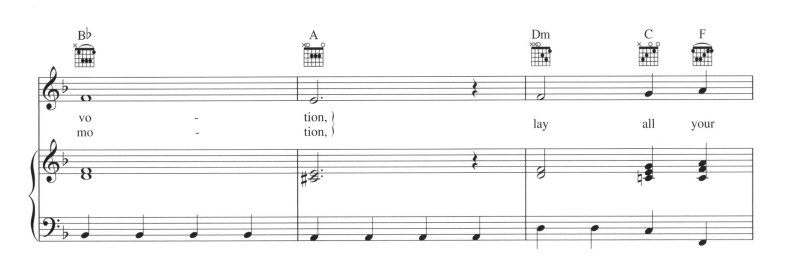

vo   -   tion,   lay   all   your
mo   -   tion,

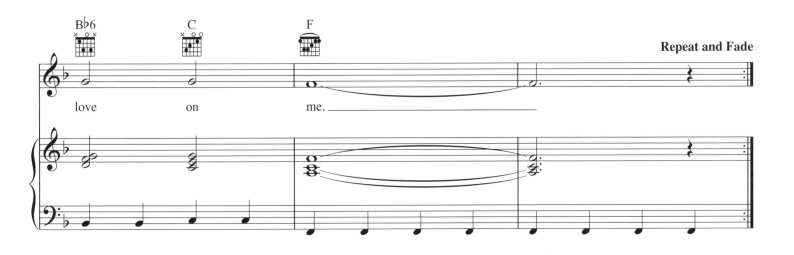

Repeat and Fade

love   on   me. _____

OUR LAST SUMMER

Words and Music by BENNY ANDERSSON
and BJÖRN ULVAEUS

The sum-mer air was soft and warm, the feel-ing right, the Par-is night did its best to please us. And stroll-ing down the E - ly - sée we had a drink in each ca - fé, and you, you talked of pol-i-tics, phi-los-o-phy and I smiled like Mo-na Li-sa.

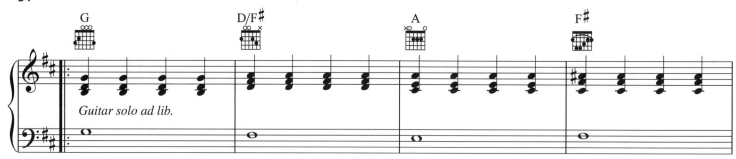

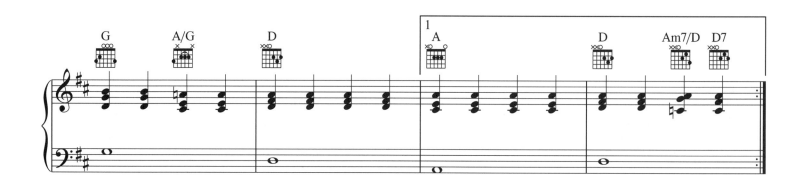

Solo ends

And now you're work-in' in a bank, a fam-'ly man, a foot-ball

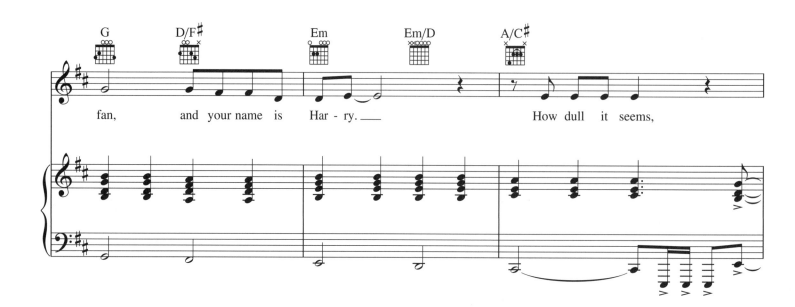

fan, and your name is Har- ry. ___ How dull it seems,

SUPER TROUPER

Words and Music by BENNY ANDERSSON
and BJÖRN ULVAEUS

GIMME! GIMME! GIMME!
(A Man After Midnight)

Words and Music by BENNY ANDERSSON
and BJÖRN ULVAEUS

Moderate Rock

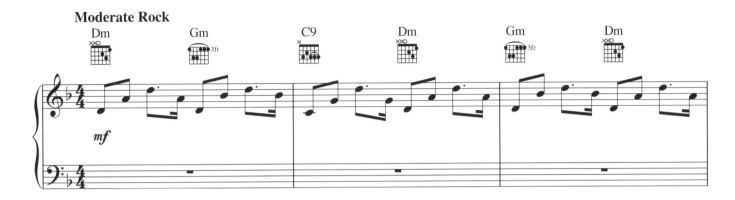

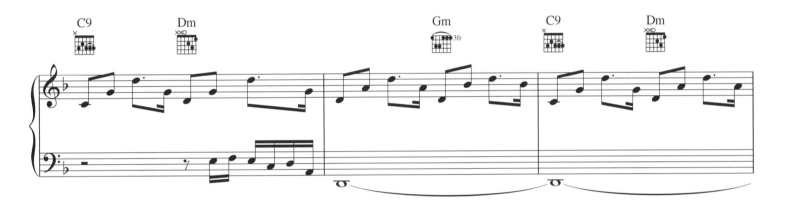

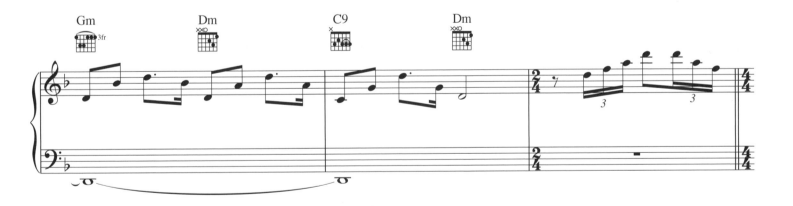

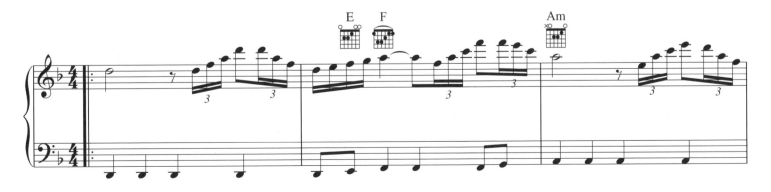

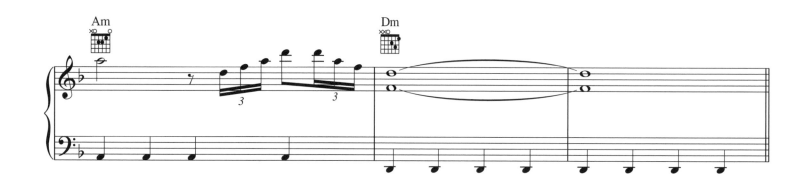

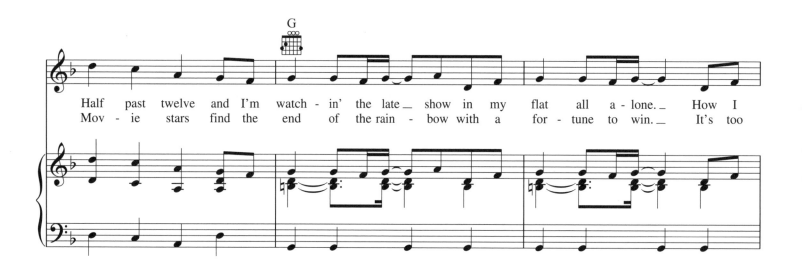

Half past twelve and I'm watch-in' the late _ show in my flat all a-lone. _ How I
Mov - ie stars find the end of the rain - bow with a for - tune to win. _ It's too

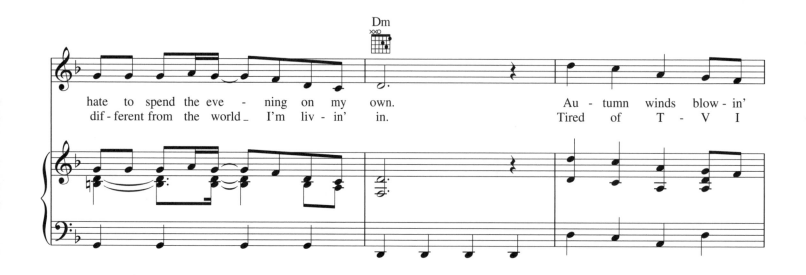

hate to spend the eve - ning on my own. _ Au - tumn winds blow-in'
dif - ferent from the world _ I'm liv - in' in. Tired of T - V I

some-bod-y help me chase the shad-ows a-way.__ Gim-me! Gim-me! Gim-me! a man__

af-ter mid-night, take__ me through the dark-ness to the break of the day.__

Repeat and Fade

THE NAME OF THE GAME

Words and Music by BENNY ANDERSSON,
BJÖRN ULVAEUS and STIG ANDERSON

SOS

Words and Music by BENNY ANDERSSON,
BJÖRN ULVAEUS and STIG ANDERSON

Strong Rock tempo

Where are those hap - py days? ___ They seem so hard ___ to find. ___
You seem so far a - way ___ though you are stand - ing near. ___

I try to reach ___ for you, ___ but you have closed ___ my mind. ___
You made me feel ___ a - live ___ but some - thing died ___ I fear. ___

VOULEZ-VOUS

Words and Music by BENNY ANDERSSON
and BJÖRN ULVAEUS

Disco

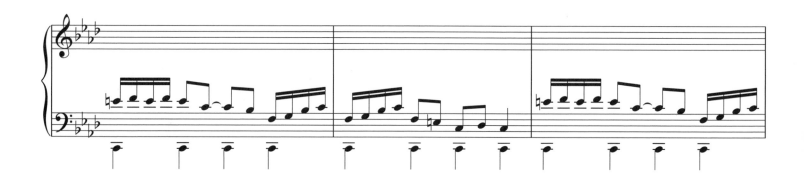

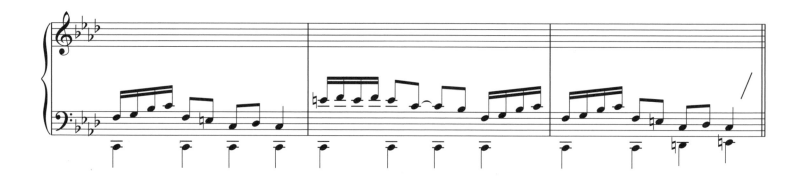

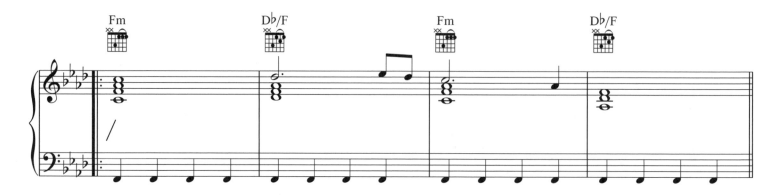

Fm   Db/F

People ev - 'ry - where, __   a sense of ex - pec - ta - tion
I know what __ you think; __   the girl means busi - ness so I'll

Fm   Db/F   Fm

hang - in' in __ the air, __   giv - in' out __ a spark, __
of - fer her __ a drink. __   Look - in' might - y proud, __

Db/F   Fm   Db/F   Fm

a - cross the room your eyes are   glow - in' in ___ the dark. __   And here we
I see you leave your ta - ble   push - in' through __ the crowd. __   I'm real - ly

C

(1., D.S.) go a - gain, __ we know the start, __ we   know the end, __
(2.) glad you came, __ you know the rules, __ you   know the game, __

noth-ing prom-ised, no re - grets. _____ Vou - lez vous, _____ ain't__ no big de - ci - sion, you__ know what to do, ____ la ques-tion c'est vou-lez vous, _____ vou - lez vous. _____

DOES YOUR MOTHER KNOW

Words and Music by BENNY ANDERSSON
and BJÖRN ULVAEUS

in your face   that your   feel - ings are driv - ing you wild, ___   ah, ___
what you mean   when you   give   me   a   flash of that   smile, ___   ah, ___

___ but girl, you're on - ly   a   child. ___
___ but girl, you're on - ly   a   child. ___

Well, I could

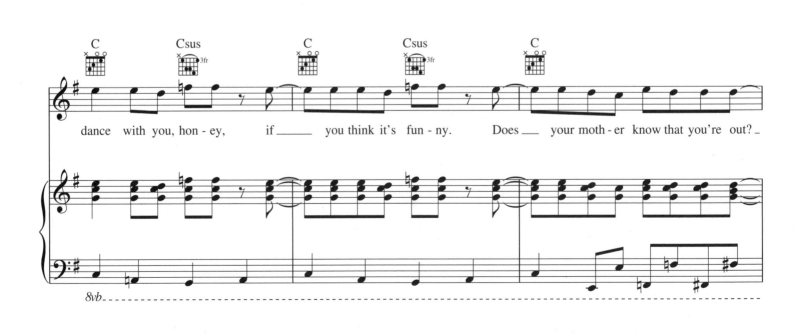

dance   with you, hon - ey,   if ___ you think it's fun - ny.   Does ___ your moth - er know that you're out? ___

And I could chat with you, ba-by, flirt___ a lit-tle may-be. Does___

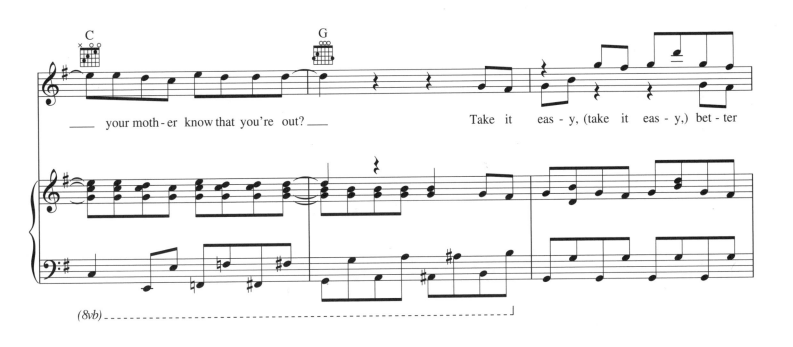

___ your moth-er know that you're out? ___ Take it eas-y, (take it eas-y,) bet-ter

slow down, girl. ___ That's no way to go. ___ (Does your moth-er know?) ___ Take it

eas - y, (take it eas - y,) try to cool it, girl.＿ Play it nice and slow.＿ (Does your

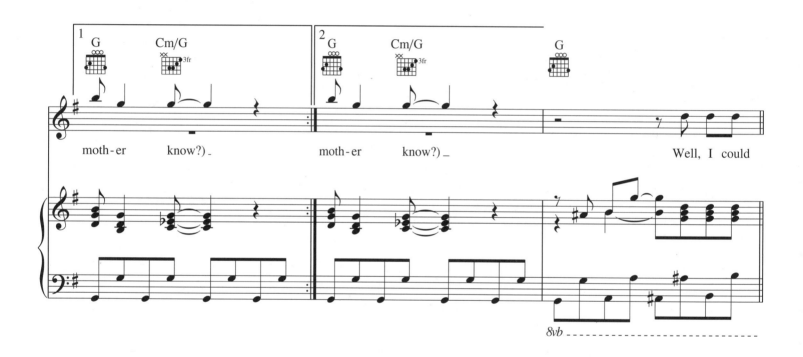

moth - er know?)＿   moth - er know?)＿   Well, I could

8vb -

dance with you, hon - ey,   if ＿ you think it's fun - ny.   Does ＿ your moth - er know that you're out? ＿

(8vb) -

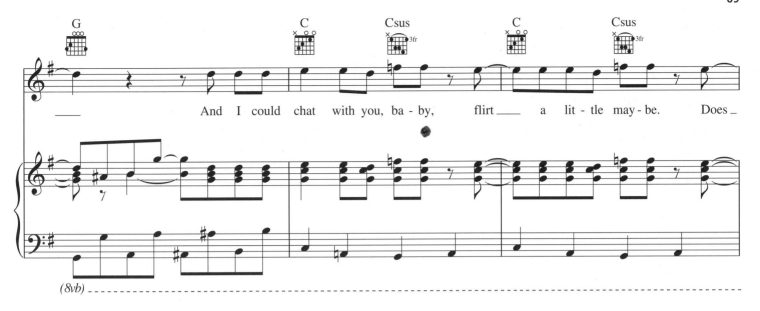

And I could chat with you, ba - by, flirt ___ a lit - tle may - be. Does ___

Repeat and Fade

___ your moth - er know that you're out? _____ Well, I could

Optional Ending

___ your moth - er know that you're out? _____

SLIPPING THROUGH MY FINGERS

Words and Music by BENNY ANDERSSON
and BJÖRN ULVAEUS

Moderately slow

School-bag in hand, __ she leaves home in the ear-ly morn-ing,
Sleep in our eyes, __ her and me at the break-fast ta-ble,

mp

With pedal

wav-ing good-bye with an ab-sent-mind-ed smile. ____
bare-ly a-wake, I let pre-cious time go by. ____

I watch her go with a surge of that well-known sad-ness,
Then when she's gone, there's that old mel-an-chol-y feel-ing

THE WINNER TAKES IT ALL

Words and Music by BENNY ANDERSSON
and BJÖRN ULVAEUS

To Coda

no more ace to play.
play - ing by the rules.
rules must be o - beyed.
no self con - fi - dence.

The win - ner takes it
The gods may throw a
The judg - es will de -
The win - ner takes it

all,
dice,
cide,

the los - er stand - ing small
their minds as cold as ice,
the likes of me a - bide,

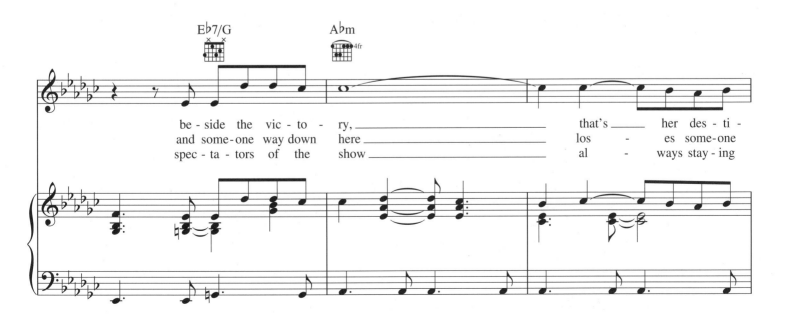

be - side the vic - to - ry, _____
and some - one way down here _____
spec - ta - tors of the show _____

that's _____ her des - ti -
los - es some - one
al - ways stay - ing

The win-ner takes it all.

Repeat and Fade

WHEN ALL IS SAID AND DONE

Words and Music by BENNY ANDERSSON
and BJÖRN ULVAEUS

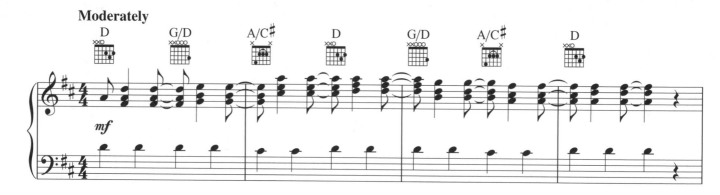

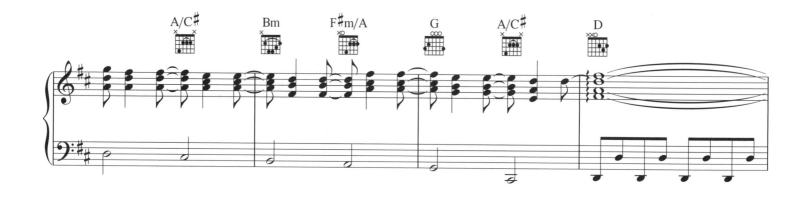

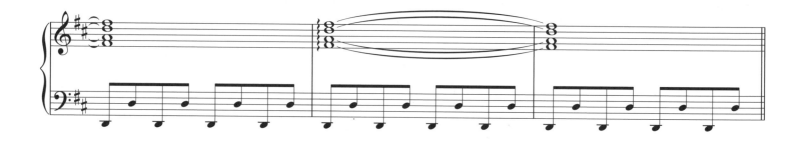

Here's to   us, _____   one   more   toast ___   and then ___   we'll   pay ___   the bill. __
In   our   lives ___   we   have   walked _   some strange ___ and   lone - ly treks, __
It's so   strange _   when you're   down ___ and ly - ing   on ___   the floor __

nei - ther you __ nor I'm __ to blame __ when all __ is said __ and done.
Nei - ther you __ nor I'm __ to blame __ when all __ is said __ and done.
There's no hur - ry an - y - more __ when all __ is said __ and done.

To Coda ⊕

D.S. al Coda

TAKE A CHANCE ON ME

Words and Music by BENNY ANDERSSON
and BJÖRN ULVAEUS

Moderate Dance beat

feel - ing down. ____ If you're all a - lone ____ when the pret - ty birds ____

____ have flown, hon - ey, I'm still free, ____ take a chance on me. ____

____ Gon - na do my ver - y best, ba - by, can't you see, ____ got - ta put me to ____

____ the test, take a chance on me. ____ If you change your mind, ____

Repeat and Fade

I HAVE A DREAM

Words and Music by BENNY ANDERSSON
and BJÖRN ULVAEUS